I0017044

Iphone 14 user guide for beginners and seniors

A comprehensive user manual to unlocking the power of the Apple smartphone series with step by step instructions,tips and tricks and expert insights.

Jackson knight

Copyright page

Copyright © 2023 by Carlos D. Gray.

All rights reserved. No part of this publication may be reproduced, distributed, or transmitted in any form or by any means, including photocopying, recording, or other electronic or mechanical methods, without the prior written permission of the publisher, except in the case of brief quotations embodied in critical reviews and certain other noncommercial uses permitted by copyright law.
For permission requests, write to the publisher at:

Carlos D. Gray @ ancientgospel2@gmail.com

Table of contents

Chapter 1: Introduction

Welcome to the exciting world of the iPhone 14, where innovation meets elegance. This user guide is designed to be your companion on this technological journey, providing you with comprehensive insights and step-by-step instructions to help you make the most out of your cutting-edge device.

Welcome to iPhone 14

Congratulations on your choice of the iPhone 14, a device that seamlessly integrates power and sophistication. The moment you unwrap your new iPhone, you embark on a journey into a realm of possibilities. The purpose of this section is to acquaint you with the device's basic components and guide you through the initial setup process.

As you hold your iPhone 14 for the first time, you'll notice its sleek design, the vibrant display that brings images to life, and the tactile responsiveness of the buttons. Take a moment to appreciate the craftsmanship that Apple has poured into this device, combining aesthetics with functionality.

To get started, locate the power button and follow the on-screen instructions to turn on your iPhone. The setup wizard will greet you, prompting you to choose your language, connect to a Wi-Fi network, and sign in with your Apple ID. If you don't have an Apple ID, don't worry; the setup process will help you create one.

Once you've completed the initial steps, the iPhone 14 will ask if you want to restore your apps and data from a previous device. If you're upgrading from an older iPhone, this is a convenient way to seamlessly transition to your new device. If not, you can choose to set up your iPhone as a new device.

Setting Up Your Device

Now that your iPhone is powered on and connected, let's delve into the essential settings to personalize your device. Navigate to the Settings app, where you can tailor your preferences, adjust display settings, and configure security options.

Customizing your home screen layout is a great way to make your iPhone work for you. You can rearrange app icons, create folders, and even choose a dynamic wallpaper that changes with the time of day. Take a moment to explore these options and make your iPhone uniquely yours.

Security is paramount, and the iPhone 14 offers advanced features to protect your data. Set up Face ID or Touch ID for a secure and convenient way to unlock your device and authorize transactions. The setup process will guide you through capturing facial data or fingerprint impressions, ensuring a seamless and secure user experience.

As you proceed through the setup, you'll encounter the option to enable Siri, your intelligent personal assistant. Well,Siri can also help you with a myriad of tasks, from sending messages even to setting reminders and so. Embrace the convenience of voice commands by allowing Siri to enhance your overall iPhone experience.

In this chapter, we've covered the initial steps of welcoming you to the iPhone 14 family and setting up your device for optimal use. As you continue reading, each chapter will delve into specific features and functionalities, guiding you towards becoming a proficient user of your iPhone 14. Get ready to unlock the full potential of your device and embark on a journey of seamless connectivity and innovation.

Chapter 2: Navigating the Interface

Welcome to the heart of your iPhone 14 experience – navigating the intuitive interface that makes using your device a breeze. This chapter will guide you through the essentials of the iPhone 14 interface, empowering you to seamlessly interact with your device and access its myriad features.

Home Screen Essentials

The home screen is your iPhone's command center, where you launch apps, view notifications, and access your favorite features. At the bottom of the screen, you'll find the Dock, a handy space to store your most-used apps. To customize it, tap and hold an app until they jiggle, then drag them into your preferred arrangement.

App icons on the home screen are more than just shortcuts. They can display information through app badges, giving you at-a-glance updates. For example, the Mail app will show the number of unread emails directly on its icon. Managing notifications is simple – swipe down from the top to access the Notification Center, where you can review and manage alerts.

But the magic doesn't stop there. A long press on app icons reveals quick actions, providing shortcuts to specific features. Try it with the Camera app to quickly capture a selfie or jump straight into video recording. This time-saving feature adds a layer of efficiency to your daily interactions.

Control Center and Notifications

Swipe up from the bottom of the screen, and you'll unveil the Control Center – a convenient hub for accessing essential settings. Adjust brightness, toggle Wi-Fi or Bluetooth, and control music playback with a few taps. Customizing the Control Center is easy; head to Settings > Control Center to add or remove shortcuts based on your preferences.

Notifications usually play a crucial role in keeping you well informed. Whether it's a missed call, a new message, or an app update, your iPhone 14 ensures you stay in the loop. Dive into Settings > Notifications to tailor how notifications appear and organize them to suit your workflow.

Mastering the art of notifications involves using grouping options and managing app-specific settings. Tame the influx of alerts by deciding which apps can break through the silent mode and which are better left for a leisurely check when you have the time.

In this section, we've covered the essentials of your iPhone 14's home screen, including customization options and efficient ways to manage notifications. The goal is to empower you with the knowledge to make your device truly yours, streamlining your digital interactions and enhancing your overall user experience.

As you become more familiar with these features, navigating your iPhone 14 will become second nature. The next chapters will explore communication features, ensuring you're ready to stay connected with friends and family effortlessly. So, keep exploring, and get ready to make your iPhone 14 an integral part of your daily life.

Chapter 3: Communication Features

Your iPhone 14 is not just a device; it's a gateway to seamless communication. In this chapter, we'll delve into the fundamental features that allow you to connect with others effortlessly, whether it's making calls or sending messages. Get ready to explore the communication capabilities that make your iPhone 14 a powerful tool for staying in touch.

Making and Receiving Calls

The cornerstone of any smartphone is its ability to make and receive calls, and the iPhone

14 takes this fundamental feature to the next level. To make a call, open the Phone app and dial the number directly or select a contact from your address book. Need to make a call quickly? Use the convenient shortcut by pressing the green phone icon on the home screen.

Answering calls is equally straightforward. When someone calls you, swipe the green phone icon to the right to answer. In order to decline/reject, just swipe the red phone icon to the left. Want to send a quick message instead? Swipe up on the message icon to access pre-set responses.

But the iPhone 14 offers more than just traditional calls. FaceTime, Apple's video and audio calling feature, enables you to connect with friends and family visually. Initiate a FaceTime call from the Phone app or directly from a contact in your address book.

Messaging Tips and Tricks

Texting has evolved into a dynamic and expressive form of communication, and the Messages app on your iPhone 14 is equipped with features to enhance your messaging experience. Start a new conversation by tapping the compose button in the Messages app or selecting a contact from your address book.

The keyboard supports predictive text, making it easier and faster to compose messages. Additionally, tap and hold the send button to access a range of effects, such as balloons or confetti, to add a touch of flair to your messages.

Emojis and stickers allow you to express yourself in creative ways. Access the emoji keyboard by tapping the smiley face icon, and explore a vast array of expressive icons. For even more personalization, use Memoji – animated avatars that mimic your facial expressions.

Group chats are a fantastic way to stay connected with multiple friends or family members simultaneously. Create a group by tapping the compose button and selecting multiple contacts. This way, you can share updates, make plans, and enjoy lively conversations with everyone in one thread.

In this section, we've explored the communication features of your iPhone 14, from traditional calls to the expressive world of messaging. As you familiarize yourself with these capabilities, your device transforms into a powerful tool for staying connected with your social circle. The subsequent chapters will guide you through mastering the iPhone 14's camera, ensuring you capture and share your precious moments seamlessly. So, keep exploring, and let your iPhone 14 become your trusted companion in the realm of communication.

Chapter 4: Mastering the Camera

Your iPhone 14 is equipped with a sophisticated camera system that goes beyond just capturing moments – it helps you create stunning visual narratives. In this chapter, we'll delve into the intricacies of the camera features, guiding you through the art of photography and video recording.

Capturing Stunning Photos

Unlock the full potential of your iPhone 14's camera by mastering the art of photography. Open the Camera app, and you're greeted with a simple yet powerful interface. The shutter button takes center stage, ready to capture your moments with a tap. But let's dive deeper.

Tap to focus: Ensure your subject is in sharp focus by tapping on the screen. The camera will adjust the focus and exposure accordingly. Experiment with different focal points to create visually engaging compositions.

Live Photos: Activate Live Photos by toggling the icon at the top of the screen. This feature captures a few seconds of audio and video before and after you take a photo, adding a delightful touch of life to your still images.

Portrait mode: Elevate your portraits by using Portrait mode. Access this feature by swiping to the right on the camera modes at the bottom of the screen. It adds a beautiful depth-of-field effect, keeping your subject sharp while artfully blurring the background.

The Night mode: Do not allow low light conditions hinder/affect your photography. When shooting in low light, the Night mode icon will appear. Tap it to enable this feature, allowing your iPhone to capture vibrant and detailed photos even in challenging lighting situations.

Editing tools: The Photos app offers a range of editing tools to enhance your photos. Explore options like adjusting brightness, adding filters, and cropping to transform your pictures into true masterpieces.

Exploring Video Recording Features

The iPhone 14's camera isn't just for photos – it's a powerful tool for creating captivating videos. Switch to video mode by swiping to the right on the camera modes. Once you're in video mode, the same principles of tapping to focus and adjusting exposure apply.

4K video recording: Elevate your videography by capturing moments in 4K resolution. Navigate to Settings > Camera > Record Video and select the highest resolution. This ensures your videos are not only memorable but also crystal clear.

Slow-motion and time-lapse: Add a cinematic touch to your videos with slow-motion and time-lapse recording. Swipe to the right until you find the desired mode, and let your creativity shine. Slow-motion is perfect for highlighting specific moments, while time-lapse can transform the ordinary into the extraordinary.

Editing videos: The Photos app allows you to edit your videos seamlessly. Trim clips, add music, and apply filters to create share-worthy content. Your iPhone 14 empowers you to be a storyteller, capturing and editing videos with ease.

As you explore the camera features of your iPhone 14, you'll discover a world of creative possibilities at your fingertips. The next chapters will guide you through personalization and settings, ensuring your device is tailored to your preferences. So, keep capturing those moments, and let your iPhone 14 be your trusted companion on your visual storytelling journey.

Chapter 5: Personalization and Settings

Your iPhone 14 is more than just a device; it's an extension of your preferences and style. This chapter will guide you through the realm of personalization and settings, empowering you to tailor your device to match your unique needs.

Customizing Your Preferences

Make your iPhone 14 truly yours by diving into the myriad customization options available. Head to the Settings app, where a world of personalization awaits. Let's start with the Display & Brightness section.

Adjust brightness: Tweak your display brightness to match your surroundings and save battery life. A brighter setting is ideal for outdoor use, while a lower setting can be gentler on the eyes in darker environments.

Text size and bold text: Enhance readability by adjusting the text size to your liking. If you prefer bolder text, enable the Bold Text option for a more pronounced and legible display.

Wallpapers: Transform the look and feel of your device by changing your wallpaper. Choose from dynamic, still, or live wallpapers to suit your mood. Access these options in the Wallpaper section of Settings.

Sounds & Haptics: Customize your iPhone's auditory experience by selecting your preferred ringtone, text tone, and vibration pattern. Express your personality through the sounds that resonate with you.

Accessibility: Tailor your device to accommodate specific needs through the Accessibility settings. From text-to-speech features to color adjustments, explore the options available to enhance the usability of your iPhone.

Security and Privacy Settings

Protecting your personal information is paramount. The iPhone 14 offers robust security and privacy settings to ensure your data remains confidential.

Face ID or Touch ID: Set up biometric authentication with Face ID or Touch ID for a secure and convenient unlocking experience. Head to Face ID & Passcode or Touch ID & Passcode in Settings to configure these features.

Passcode: Strengthen your device's security with a custom passcode. Select a combination that is memorable for you yet presents a challenge for others to decipher. Periodically changing your passcode enhances your security by introducing an additional layer of protection.

Privacy settings: Navigate to the Privacy section in Settings to review and manage app permissions. Decide which apps have access to your location, contacts, photos, and other sensitive information. Your iPhone puts you in control of your privacy.

App Tracking Transparency: Empower yourself with control over app tracking. In the Privacy section, explore the App Tracking Transparency setting, allowing you to choose whether apps can track your activity across other companies' apps and websites.

In this section, we've explored the vast array of personalization and security settings on your iPhone 14. As you tailor your device to align with your preferences and ensure the security of your data, you're actively shaping a personalized and secure digital experience. The upcoming chapters will guide you through maximizing productivity with apps and exploring advanced features. So, continue to make your iPhone 14 uniquely yours, and let it seamlessly integrate into your lifestyle.

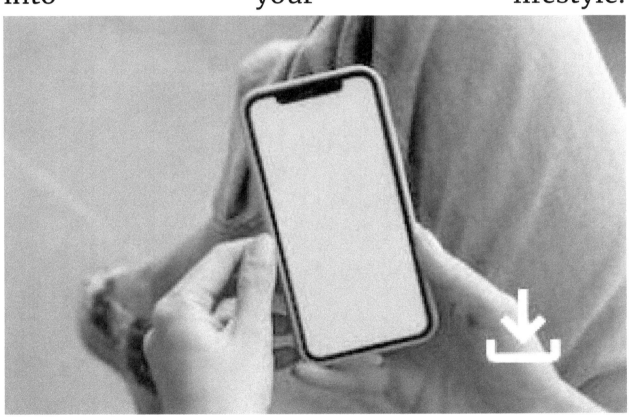

Chapter 6: Productivity and Apps

Your iPhone 14 isn't just a communication and entertainment device; it's a powerful tool for productivity. In this chapter, we'll explore the world of apps and features that can enhance your efficiency, creativity, and overall productivity.

Getting the Most from Productivity Apps

The App Store on your iPhone 14 is a treasure trove of productivity apps designed to streamline your tasks and make your daily life more organized. Let's dive into a few key categories of productivity apps and how they can elevate your efficiency:

Note-Taking Apps: Explore apps like Apple Notes or third-party options such as Evernote or Microsoft OneNote to jot down ideas, create to-do lists, and organize your thoughts. These apps often offer features like checklists, image embedding, and synchronization across devices.

Calendar Apps: Leverage the power of calendar apps like Apple Calendar or Google Calendar to keep track of your schedule, appointments, and important dates. Set reminders, create events, and sync with other devices to stay seamlessly organized.

Task Management Apps: Boost your productivity with task management apps like Todoist, Microsoft To Do, or Things. These apps enable you to create and prioritize tasks, set deadlines, and organize your responsibilities effectively.

Document Scanning Apps: Transform your iPhone into a portable scanner with apps like Adobe Scan or Microsoft Office Lens. Capture documents, receipts, or whiteboard notes, and convert them into shareable PDFs or images.

App Store Recommendations

Navigate to the App Store, and you'll discover a vast array of apps tailored to your interests and needs. The "Today" tab features curated lists, app spotlights, and useful tips to help you discover new and noteworthy apps. The "Apps" and "Games" tabs offer categories ranging from education to health and fitness, ensuring you find apps that align with your lifestyle.

App ratings and reviews provide valuable insights into the user experience. Before downloading an app, take a moment to read reviews and assess ratings to ensure it meets your expectations. Additionally, explore the "Updates" tab to keep your apps current with the latest features and improvements.

Consider exploring app subscriptions for enhanced features and an ad-free experience. Many apps offer premium versions with additional functionalities that can further elevate your user experience.

As you navigate the world of productivity apps on your iPhone 14, remember to tailor your app selection to your specific needs. Whether you're a student, professional, or someone who simply wants to stay organized, the App Store has a wealth of options to enhance your productivity and simplify your daily tasks.

The upcoming chapters will guide you through advanced features, unlocking the potential of Face ID and Touch ID, and exploring the immersive world of augmented reality experiences on your iPhone 14. So, continue to explore, customize, and make the most of your device as it seamlessly integrates into your daily routine.

Chapter 7: Advanced Features

Your iPhone 14 is equipped with advanced features that go beyond the basics, offering you a more sophisticated and personalized user experience. In this chapter, we'll explore the capabilities of Face ID and Touch ID, unlocking new levels of security and convenience, as well as delve into the immersive world of augmented reality.

Face ID and Touch ID

Face ID:

Face ID is Apple's facial recognition technology that provides a secure and seamless way to unlock your iPhone, authorize app purchases, and more. To set up Face ID, navigate to Settings > Face ID & Passcode. Follow the on-screen instructions to capture your facial features, creating a biometric profile unique to you.

Once Face ID is configured, unlocking your iPhone is as simple as looking at it. The TrueDepth camera system scans your face with precision, even in low-light conditions. Face ID adapts to changes in your appearance over time, ensuring a consistent and reliable user experience.

Beyond unlocking your device, Face ID enhances security in various apps and services. From banking apps to password managers, Face ID provides a secure authentication method, reducing the reliance on passwords.

Touch ID:

If you prefer a tactile method of authentication, the iPhone 14 continues to support Touch ID, Apple's fingerprint recognition technology. Head to Settings >

Touch ID & Passcode to set up Touch ID. Follow the prompts to register your fingerprint, allowing you to unlock your device and authorize transactions with a simple touch.

Touch ID is not only convenient but also versatile. It seamlessly integrates with the App Store, allowing you to make purchases with a touch of your finger. Additionally, it enhances security for third-party apps that support fingerprint authentication.

Choosing between Face ID and Touch ID is a matter of personal preference. Some users appreciate the hands-free convenience of Face ID, while others prefer the familiarity of Touch ID. Whichever method you choose, rest assured that your iPhone 14 is equipped with advanced biometric security.

Augmented Reality Experiences

The iPhone 14 opens the door to a captivating world of augmented reality (AR), where digital elements blend seamlessly with the real world through your device's camera and sensors. Explore these AR experiences to add a touch of magic to your daily life:

AR Apps:

Visit the App Store's AR category to discover a variety of apps that leverage augmented reality. From measuring distances with your camera to trying on virtual furniture in your living room, AR apps bring a new dimension to your iPhone experience.

AR Games:

Immerse yourself in interactive gaming experiences with AR games. These games utilize your physical surroundings, turning your living room into a virtual playground. Whether it's solving puzzles or battling virtual creatures, AR games provide an engaging and dynamic form of entertainment.

ARKit Development:

For those interested in creating their own AR experiences, Apple's ARKit provides a platform for developers to build innovative apps. The possibilities range from educational tools to interactive storytelling, allowing users to explore and interact with digital content in real-world environments.

As you explore the advanced features of Face ID, Touch ID, and augmented reality on your iPhone 14, you're tapping into a realm of possibilities that enhance both security and entertainment. The subsequent chapters will delve into troubleshooting common issues, providing support resources, and offering tips and tricks to make the most of your device. So, continue to embrace the advanced capabilities of your iPhone 14, making it an integral part of

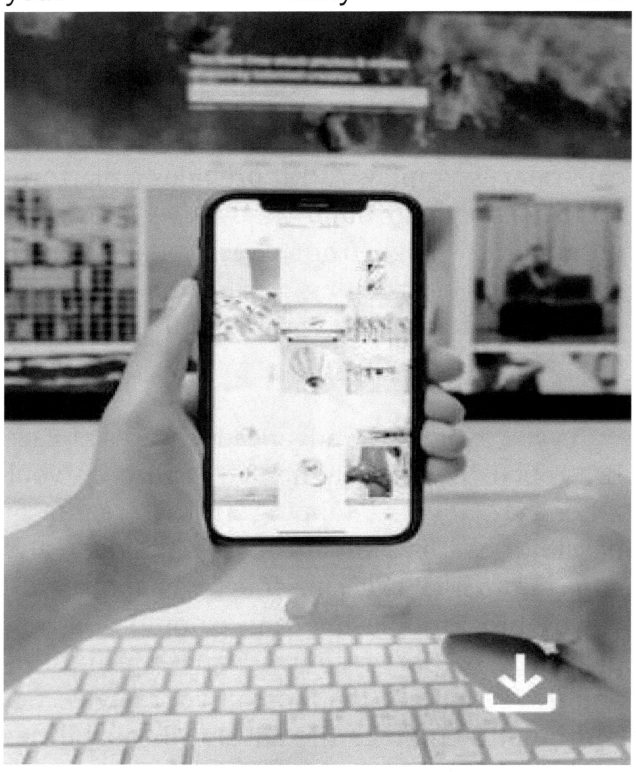

Chapter 8: Troubleshooting and Support

While your iPhone 14 is designed to provide a seamless and reliable experience, occasional challenges may arise. In this chapter, we'll explore common issues users might encounter, offer troubleshooting solutions, and guide you to valuable support resources to ensure your device operates smoothly.

Common Issues and Solutions

Battery Draining Quickly:

If you notice your battery depleting faster than usual, start by checking which apps consume the most power. Head to Settings > Battery to view battery usage details. Consider closing background apps, adjusting screen brightness, and enabling Low Power Mode when necessary. If the issue persists, restarting your iPhone or updating to the latest iOS version may resolve the problem.

Wi-Fi Connection Problems:

If you're experiencing Wi-Fi connectivity issues, begin by ensuring Wi-Fi is enabled in Settings. Restart your router, and try connecting to the network again. If the problem persists, "Forget" the Wi-Fi network in Settings and reconnect by entering the password. Alternatively, resetting network settings may solve more complex connectivity issues.

App Crashes:

Apps occasionally crash due to bugs or compatibility issues. Ensure your apps are updated to the latest versions through the App Store. If a specific app consistently crashes, consider uninstalling and reinstalling it. Restarting your iPhone can also resolve temporary glitches that contribute to app crashes.

Slow Performance:

If your iPhone is running sluggishly, optimizing performance can be achieved by clearing storage space. Delete unused apps, photos, and videos, and consider transferring data to iCloud or an external device. Additionally, restarting your device periodically can refresh its performance.

Where to Find Help

Apple Support App:
The Apple Support app is a valuable resource for troubleshooting and assistance. Download it from the App Store to access articles, tutorials,

and the option to chat with Apple Support. The app can also initiate remote diagnostics to identify and resolve issues.

Online Support Resources:

Apple's official website offers an extensive support section with articles, user guides, and community forums. Visit support.apple.com for comprehensive troubleshooting guides, software updates, and answers to frequently asked questions.

Genius Bar Appointments:

For in-person assistance, schedule an appointment at the Apple Store's Genius Bar. The Apple Support app facilitates appointment booking, allowing you to choose a convenient time to receive personalized assistance from Apple experts.

Community Forums:

Engage with the Apple community through online forums like the Apple Support Communities. Here, users share experiences, troubleshoot together, and offer advice. It's a collaborative space to find solutions and connect with fellow iPhone users.

Contacting Apple Support:

If you prefer direct assistance, Apple Support offers phone and chat support. Contact details are available on the official website. Apple Support representatives can guide you through troubleshooting steps and provide tailored solutions.

Navigating common issues and seeking support ensures that your iPhone 14 remains a reliable and efficient companion. The troubleshooting solutions mentioned in this chapter, coupled with the various support resources available, empower you to overcome challenges and maintain a positive user experience.

As we conclude this chapter, the next section will unveil a treasure trove of tips and tricks, revealing hidden gems and shortcuts to elevate your iPhone 14 usage. So, continue exploring and troubleshooting, knowing that assistance is readily available to enhance your device experience.

Chapter 9: Tips and Tricks

Welcome to the treasure trove of Tips and Tricks, where we unveil hidden gems and shortcuts to elevate your iPhone 14 usage. In this chapter, we'll explore lesser-known features, time-saving hacks, and ways to maximize your device's capabilities.

Hidden Gems and Shortcuts

Quick Access to Camera:

Capture the moment swiftly by accessing the camera from the lock screen. Swipe left on the lock screen, and the camera app instantly opens, allowing you to capture spontaneous events without navigating through menus.

One-Handed Keyboard:

Make typing more comfortable with the one-handed keyboard feature. Hold down the globe or emoji icon on the keyboard, then select either the left or right-handed keyboard layout for easier one-handed typing.

Shake to Undo:

Made a mistake while typing or editing text? Give your iPhone a gentle shake, and an "Undo Typing" option will appear. This quick gesture simplifies the process of undoing unintended actions.

Magnifier Feature:

Turn your iPhone into a magnifying glass by enabling the Magnifier feature. Head to Settings > Accessibility > Magnifier and toggle it on. Triple-press the side or home button (depending on your device model) to activate the Magnifier and zoom in on small text or objects.

Customized Text Replacement:

Save time by creating custom text replacements for frequently used phrases. Navigate to Settings > General > Keyboard > Text Replacement. Add a phrase and its corresponding shortcut, and your iPhone will automatically expand the shortcut into the full phrase when typed.

Maximizing Battery Life

Optimize Battery Charging:

Extend your battery's lifespan by enabling Optimized Battery Charging. Found in Settings > Battery > Battery Health, this feature helps slow down battery aging by reducing the time your iPhone spends fully charged. It learns your daily charging habits and ensures your device is fully charged when you need it.

Background App Refresh:

Conserve battery by managing Background App Refresh. Go to Settings > General > Background App Refresh and disable it for apps that don't require constant updates. This prevents apps from refreshing content in the background, preserving battery life.

Low Power Mode:

When your battery is running low, activate Low Power Mode for a temporary boost in battery life. Access it quickly by swiping down on the Control Center and tapping the battery icon. This mode reduces background activity, fetches new mail less frequently, and disables some visual effects.

Location Services Optimization:

Enhance battery efficiency by managing Location Services. Head to Settings > Privacy > Location Services. Choose either to disable

Location Services entirely or customize the settings for individual apps. Select "While Using the App" to allow location access only when the app is in use.

As you incorporate these tips and tricks into your iPhone 14 usage, you'll discover a more efficient and personalized user experience. From capturing spontaneous moments with quick camera access to optimizing battery life, these insights aim to enhance your daily interactions with your device.

The final chapter awaits, offering a comprehensive conclusion to your iPhone 14 user guide journey. It will summarize key takeaways, reinforce essential concepts, and encourage you to continue exploring and making the most of your iPhone 14. So, let's embark on the final section, celebrating the knowledge gained and looking forward to the endless possibilities your device holds.

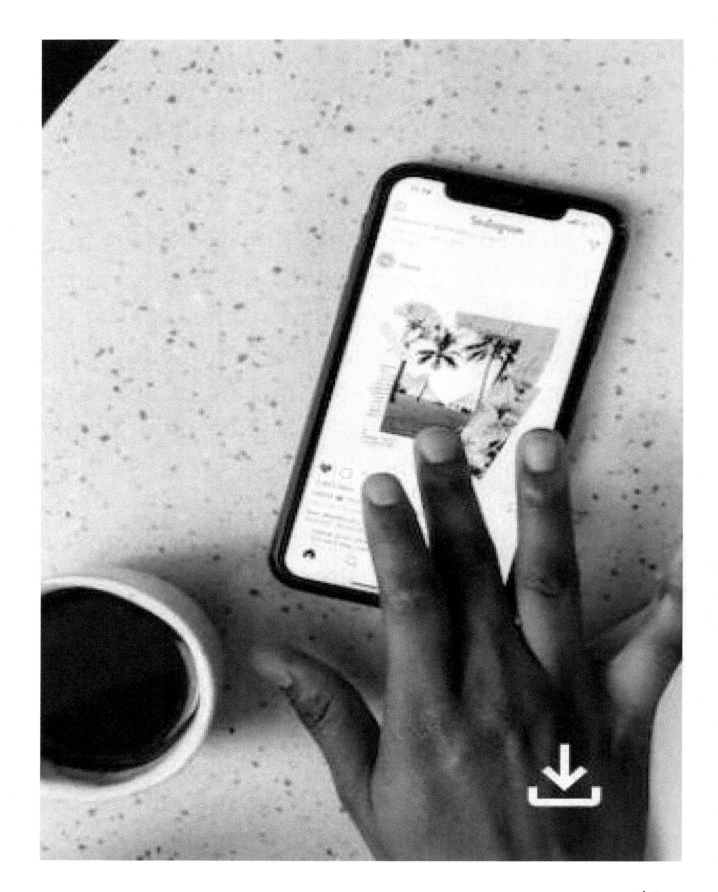

Chapter 10: Conclusion

Congratulations on completing your journey through this comprehensive iPhone 14 User Guide! As we conclude, let's recap the key takeaways, reinforce essential concepts, and encourage you to continue exploring the endless possibilities your device holds.

1 Key Takeaways

Throughout this guide, you've delved into the fundamental aspects of your iPhone 14, from the initial setup to advanced features and tips for optimizing your user experience. Here are some key takeaways to remember:

- **Mastering the Basics**: Understanding the foundational elements, such as navigating the interface, making calls, and sending messages, forms the basis of a proficient iPhone user.

- **Capturing Moments**: The camera features of your iPhone 14 are a gateway to creative expression. From capturing stunning photos to exploring video recording capabilities, your device empowers you to be a visual storyteller.

- **Personalization and Settings**: Tailoring your device through customization and adjusting security settings ensures your iPhone aligns with your preferences while safeguarding your personal information.

- **Productivity and Apps**: Explore the App Store for productivity apps that can enhance your efficiency and organization. Your iPhone is not just a communication tool; it's a powerful ally in managing your daily tasks.

- **Advanced Features:** Embrace the convenience and security offered by Face ID and Touch ID. Dive into the immersive world of augmented reality to experience a blend of digital and real-world elements.

- **Troubleshooting and Support:** Familiarize yourself with common issues and troubleshooting solutions. Know where to find support resources, whether through the Apple Support app, online forums, or in-person Genius Bar appointments.

- **Tips and Tricks:** Uncover hidden gems and shortcuts to streamline your iPhone 14 usage. From quick camera access to battery optimization, these tips enhance your device experience.

Reinforcing Essential Concepts

- **Regular Updates**: Keep your iPhone's software up to date. Regular updates not only provide new features but also enhance security and fix bugs. Navigate to Settings > General > Software Update to check for the latest iOS version.

- **Data Backup:** Safeguard your data by regularly backing up your iPhone. Utilize iCloud or connect to your computer and use iTunes to ensure your photos, contacts, and other essential information are secure.

- **User Support:** If you encounter challenges or have questions, don't hesitate to seek support. The Apple Support app, online resources, and community forums are valuable tools to assist you in troubleshooting and gaining insights.

Continuing Your Exploration

Your iPhone 14 is a powerful and versatile device, and your journey doesn't end with this guide. Continue exploring the ever-expanding capabilities, experimenting with new apps, and staying curious about software updates and features.

As technology evolves, your iPhone will evolve with it. Stay informed about the latest advancements, engage with the vibrant Apple community, and embrace the continuous learning experience that comes with owning and using your device.

In conclusion, your iPhone 14 is not just a phone; it's a gateway to connectivity, creativity, and efficiency. Use it to capture memories, stay connected with loved ones, and navigate the digital landscape with confidence.

Thank you for choosing this guide as your companion in mastering your iPhone 14. May your journey with your device be filled with discovery, productivity, and joy. Happy exploring! If you enjoyed reading this book please give us 5 star on Amazon Kdp

Thanks a lot, we love you

www.ingramcontent.com/pod-product-compliance
Lightning Source LLC
LaVergne TN
LVHW081804050326

832903LV00027B/2094

9798868052903